THE BIRTHDAY COOKOUT

Email: akosuaobuobiwrites@gmail.com

ISBN: 9798869301536

"Mummy, is it my birthday yet?" Krystle asks her mum. "Not yet honey, it's five days away". Krystle follows her mum around the house as she cleans, helping to fold clothes. Ever since the month of June began, she asks everyday whether her birthday has arrived.

Daddy Long hands Krystle a big calendar to place in her room and circle her 'big day,' cancelling each day before it until it finally arrives.

Krystle is elated. "Finally!" She exclaims, "An activity that sounds like fun."

Maame Ama, Krystle's mum laughs and says to Daddy Long, "This will not last; she will be back in no time asking if it's her birthday yet."
Daddy Long lets out a sigh, "Well, at least we get today off". They both laugh.

Daddy Long lets out a sigh, "Well, at least we get today off". They both laugh.
Maame Ama makes arrangements with a well known caterer in the community to plan meals for her daughter's birthday celebration. All is well as she ticks off caterer from her 'to-do' list. Now the drinks for the celebration is next, she reaches out to the famous barista and mixologist - Cimpe - to find out if he is available on the date to make some mocktails for the kids.

Cimpe confirms availability and Maame Ama is pleased with herself. "Two down, one to go," she whispers as she searches for the contact number of Ish, the guy responsible for kids parties' decor. Ish also confirms his availability.
With confirmations from these three, Maame Ama is feeling like the best event planner in Kurase.

"Mummy, why has my birthday kept so long in coming?" Krystle asks her mum early in the morning as she walks into her bedroom, greets and sits at the edge of the bed.
Maame Ama, with tired eyes, rolls them at Daddy K and he responds, "Sweetheart, have you checked today's date off the calendar?"

"Yes dad, I have but it still reads two days more."
Daddy K tells Krystle to be patient as everything is in place to make her birthday a memorable one.

Later that evening, Maame Ama receives a call from the caterer.
"Oh no!" Maame Ama is heard saying loudly. Daddy K and Krystle both rush to the room to find out what the problem is. Maame Ama has a look of worry and sadness written all over her face. The caterer cancelled on her due to an emergency.

While Maame Ama ponders over what to do, there is a loud honk. Krystle is jumping up and down happily; her cousins have arrived for her birthday. Cousins J, Kim, Mampi, Kojo, Adom, Frimpong and Little Akosua along with Grandma Manu have all arrived at Kurase from Akaa. Maame Akosua, Aunty Afia, Daddy Yoo, Uncle Shushu, Akora, Opuni Foodie and Grandpa Hoden follow up as Daddy Long ushers them into his villa.

Now more than ever, the pressure is on for Maame Ama, even as she smiles and welcomes her family and guests, she is sweating and thinking hard on what to do. While all the guests settled in, Maame Ama goes upstairs to find a solution to the impending problem. Just as she sits on her bed, she hears a loud beep from her phone; she receives a text message from the barista and mixologist saying he can't make it.

Maame Ama slumps in the couch. Maame Akosua comes in to find her seated with a sad looking face and asks, "What is wrong Ama? Why do you look so sad?"
Maame Ama tells Maame Akosua everything that has transpired between her and the caterer, then she proceeds to show her the text message that just came in from the barista and mixologist.

Maame Akosua listens with intent. She tells Maame Ama she might have a solution. Maame Ama's eyes widen with anticipation. Maame Akosua continues; "There is no need to cancel the birthday party when I'm here, we can have an amazing cookout, we just need to come up with a menu and rush to the market."

Maame Ama's face suddenly lights up. She hugs Maame Akosua tightly and says thank you from the depths of her heart. Maame Akosua rallies her team; she calls on the entire family to prepare for an emergency cookout. She calls for suggestions on what to prepare.

Little Akosua, Krystle's cousin, suggests making a **burger** and serving with **passion mojito**. Cousin J opts for 'kelewele' served with nuts and **mango mojito**. Cousin Kim says she would love a **vanilla milkshake.**
Kojo wants a **banana peanut butter smoothie.** Cousins Frimpong and Adom want **grilled chicken.**

"Now it's time to hear from Grandma Manu and Grandpa Hoden," says Maame Akosua. Grandpa wants '***wrewre*** **' soup with rice balls** and Grandma wants **'*banku*' and okro soup.**

The uncles are not left out of suggestions. Uncle Opuni 'foodie' goes first as he suggests '***waakye***'. Uncle Akora says there is no party that would be fun without 'Ghana **Jollof**' and **salad** and they all burst out laughing.

Uncle Shushu and Aunty Afia opted for **Yam and '*Kontomire*' stew.**

"That seems like a lot of meals but considering the number of guests being invited, they are just perfect," said Maame Ama.

The three women; Maame Ama, Maame Akosua and Aunty Afia left for the market leaving the children with the Uncles, Daddy Long and the grandparents.

Soon, Uncle Opuni 'foodie' started searching for snacks in the fridge. He bumped into Daddy Long searching through cabinets for snacks and they both burst out laughing. It seems everyone is hungry.

The party is only two days away, the women will return from the market and put things in place for their *'mise en place'* the next day.

Little Akosua enters the kitchen with Kim and Krystle to put something together for a quick lunch. They find Yam and Gari displayed on the counter, they decide to prepare **fried yam and ground pepper,** as well as **'chicken gari fotor'.**

FRIED YAM & GROUND PEPPER SAUCE

Ingredients:

- 1 tuber of Yam
- Salt to taste
- 4 medium sized tomatoes
- 2 medium sized onions
- 4 Habanero peppers
- Oil

METHOD:

Peel yam and slice into pieces of desired shape

Wash thoroughly until clean

Put them in a bowl and pour water on the yam

Sprinkle salt to taste and allow to sit for a few minutes

Pour oil into a pan and heat

Fry pieces of yam by placing them into the oil gently so it doesn't splash

Take the fried yams out when they are crispy

Fry on medium heat so they can cook on the inside, not too high to prevent burning, not too low to prevent yam from being soggy with oil

Grind onions and pepper

Add tomatoes and grind

Add salt to taste

Serve

CHICKEN 'GARI FOTOR':

Ingredients:

- Gari 500g
- Chicken thighs deboned and cut into pieces 500g
- Tomato paste 1 cup
- Fresh tomatoes 5 medium sizes
- Onions 2 large sizes
- 2 large size habanero pepper
- Garlic 2 coves
- Ginger thumb size
- Turmeric
- Vegetables of choice; bell peppers, onions, carrots, cabbage
- All purpose seasoning
- Oil

METHOD:
Place chicken pieces in a pan on heat
Chop half of an onion into pieces and add
Grate garlic and ginger and add to it
Add 1 tsp turmeric and 1 tbsp all purpose seasoning, salt to taste
Give it a stir and allow to cook
Fry the chicken and set aside
Chop the rest of the onions and peppers and fry in the oil
Add tomato paste and stir frequently, allow to cook until it gets dark
Blend fresh tomatoes and add to it, stir
Allow to cook for a while and add chicken stock and stir
Season to taste, allow to cook until its thick
Stir in fried chicken pieces and turn off
Dice vegetables; onions, carrots, bell peppers, cabbages Into large chunks
Add chopped vegetables to the stew and stir, add the gari and mix well.
NB: Fetch a portion of stew and put aside before including chopped vegetables and Gari. This will enable you to add on if the Gari makes the stew a bit dry.

The women return home and find everyone in a happy mood with the kitchen smelling amazing. They find that the men and kids have eaten all the lunch prepared by the girls and so Maame Akosua decides to prepare lunch for herself and the other women, grandma and grandpa. She decides to make **beans and fried ripe plantain.**

INGREDIENTS:

- **1 cup Black-eyed beans**
- **5 fingers ripe plantain**
- **Salt to taste**
- **Frying oil**
- **1 cup palm oil**
- **1 small size onion**
- **Gari (optional)**

METHOD:
Wash the beans and take out impurities
Add 6 cups water to the beans and boil in a pan, add salt to taste
Allow the beans to cook until soft with the water around it being thick
Cut the ripe plantain into desirable sizes wash, place them in a bowl of water and sprinkle salt to taste
Heat oil and fry the plantains until golden brown
In another pan, heat the palm oil and slice onions and fry in it
To serve, dish out the beans and sprinkle the palm oil with fried onions and stir, add the fried plantains as accompaniment
Sprinkle Gari in the beans and stir

The next day, Maame Akosua brings the menu she designed for Maame Ama to have a look;

MENU:
Mocktails and Drinks; Mango Mojito & Passion Mojito, Peanut Butter Smoothie and Vanilla Milkshake
Snacks; Peanut butter Burgers and Fries, Kelewele and Nuts
Main Meals; Rice Balls and Wrewre Soup, Banku and Okro Soup, Waakye with stew and shito, Jollof Rice and Salad, Yam and Kontomire Stew, Grilled chicken

Everything seems to be in order as the women begin their '*mise en place*' in preparation for the big day tomorrow.

The children are having so much fun playing, the men are having a loud discussion about football, while grandma and grandpa are watching the news.

The decoration team arrive with a truckload of decoration items to setup. Soon, the men are called to help set up the barbeque station for the grilled chicken. The yard for the cookout is beginning to look incredible. Now, the children want to be part of the cooking as the setup seems inviting

"Happy Birthday Krystle!" a voice is heard shouting from the kids' room. Krystle wakes up with a wide smile. All the children gather around her to sing a happy birthday song for her.

Meanwhile, Maame Akosua, Maame Ama and Aunty Afia have been up all night getting the meals ready. They look exhausted. The yard smells amazing.

Grandma and Grandpa are up and helping the kids to get ready and have a light breakfast. Daddy and uncles have began the barbeque, the smoke from the grilled chicken goes up the extractor.

Chaffing Dishes are being arranged on tables, glasses and disposable cups are lined up on another corner, Soup bowls, plates, spoons, forks, toothpicks, tissues are all carefully displayed.

Little Akosua comes around to inspect the meals and send a report to the girls. Everything looks so good. She first sees the 'wrewre soup' boiling in a pot and wonders how it was made, it smelled amazing. Maame Akosua offers to lecture her daughter on how each meal was prepared.

"WREWRE" SOUP is also known as musk melon seeds soup.

Ingredients

- 4 cups musk melon seeds
- 2 kg hard chicken pieces
- 4 large size onions
- 8 large size fresh tomatoes
- 6 Habanero peppers
- All purpose seasoning
- ¼ shrimp powder
- Salt to taste
- 3 quarts Water

METHOD

Toast the musk melon seeds by pouring into a pan on low heat, occasionally stir to prevent burning

Set aside and allow to cool

Blend with 1 quart of water and strain

Blend the residue with another quart of water and strain

Wash the chicken and place in a pan

peel onions and wash with tomatoes and peppers and add to the chicken

Add 2 tbsps of seasoning, shrimp powder and salt to taste

Add the strained musk melon seeds liquid and turn on the heat

Allow it to boil until the onions soften

Take out the onions, pepper and tomatoes and blend with the remaining 1 quart water

Add to the boiling soup

Add salt to taste and allow it to cook

Simmer when you see oil from the seeds settle at the top

Serve hot and eat warm.

RICE BALLS

Ingredients:
- **4 cups Rice**
- **10 cups of water**

METHOD:
   Boil rice on medium heat
   Use a wooden spoon to press rice to the sides of the pan until you have a paste like texture.
   Scoop and serve with soup of your choice.
NB: For smaller portions, divide recipe in half.

e Akosua moves to the Banku and Okro soup beautifully displayed in cauldron pots and asks her mum about the preparation method.

'BANKU' & OKRO SOUP

BANKU is a local Ghanaian dish made by combining corn dough and cassava dough with water on heat and forming it into balls.

Ingredients:

- Cassava dough 500g
- Corn dough 500g
- Okro (chopped into pieces) 500g
- 4 large size onions
- 6 Habanero pepper
- 2 cups palm oil
- 2 large size Smoked Mackerels
- 2 kg fresh goat meat
- Cowhide 500g
- 250g salted beef
- ¼ cup shrimp powder
- 5 pieces scalions
- Bell peppers
- 250g mixed seafood
- All purpose seasoning
- Water

BANKU

METHOD

Mix the corn dough and cassava dough with 2 quarts of water and strain through a sieve

Add salt to taste and pour into a cauldron pot or any pot of choice

Turn on heat and stir until it thickens and forms a paste

Press out all knots while stirring

Sprinkle water and allow to cook while turning

Leave to cook, serve with okro soup.

OKRO SOUP
METHOD
- Place chopped okro, chopped scallions and chopped bell peppers in a pan, add a pint of water and turn on low heat
- Allow to boil for slime to develop and turn off heat, set aside
- In another pan, place washed goat, salted beef and cow hide
- Add 2 tbsps all purpose seasoning, blended paste of 1 onion, 3 peppers, water and salt to taste, heat
- Heat palm oil in another pan, slice 1 onion and fry in the oil
- Blend the remaining 2 onions with the 3 peppers left and pour into the oil
- De-bone mackerel and set aside
- As the stew cooks, check on the tenderness of the meat, add frozen seafood and when cooked, pour meat and stock into stew when ready, stir
- Add mackerel to the cooked stew
- Add cooked okro to the stew and allow to simmer for about 2 minutes and turn off heat
- Serve with banku

'WAAKYE', STEW AND 'SHITO'

Waakye is a local Ghanaian dish made up of rice and beans, mostly cooked with sorghum leaves to give it a rich color.

Shito is a black pepper sauce of Ghanaian origin served as an accompaniment to variety of meals.

Ingredients

- Black eyed-beans 4 cups
- Sorghum leaves
- 6 cups rice
- Water
- Salt
- Coconut Milk (optional)

METHOD

Boil beans until water thickens around it and it gets soft

Add salt to taste and pour coconut milk into it

Add washed rice to it and add sorghum leaves and more water and allow to cook

SHITO

Ingredients:

- Dry herrings fish powder 1 cup
- Shrimp powder 2 cups
- Onions 5 medium size
- Dry red chilli 10 pieces
- 2 large ginger pieces
- 1 tbsp cloves
- Oil 1 liter
- Salt
- 1 Smoked mackerel

METHOD

Peel onions and ginger and cut into chunks, wash them with the peppers and cloves

Blend them with half a liter of oil

De-bone mackerel break into small pieces, add half into the blender and continue blending with the onion mix

Pour oil into a pan and heat

Add a few slices of onions and fry, add the rest of the mackerel pieces and continue frying

Pour in your blended mix

Occasionally give it a stir

Allow to cook until it darkens

Pour your fish powder into it and stir

Add your shrimp powder, salt to taste

Continue cooking, stirring occasionally until it darkens

'WAAKYE' STEW

Ingredients

- Cow Meat
- 8 medium size fresh tomatoes
- 3 medium size onions
- 3 habanero pepper
- Ginger powder
- Garlic powder
- All purpose seasoning
- Salt
- 500g tomato paste
- Oil

METHOD

Wash cow meat

Season meat with chopped onions, garlic powder, ginger powder, all purpose seasoning and salt

Add water and cook until meat is tender

Fry meat

Slice onions and fry in oil

Add tomato paste

Blend onions and pepper and add to the oil

Add blended fresh tomatoes

Stir and add the meat stock, cover and allow to cook

Add the fried meat

Simmer until its ready

'JOLLOF' RICE AND SALAD

JOLLOF is of West African origin; a combination of stew cooked together with rice.

Ingredients

- 6 cups of rice
- 10 medium size fresh tomatoes
- 4 medium size onions
- 500g tomato paste
- 6 large size habanero peppers
- Thumb size ginger
- 2 kg soft chicken drumsticks
- Coconut milk 200ml (opt)
- Oil
- Aniseed
- Bell peppers
- Shrimp powder ¼ cup
- All purpose seasoning

METHOD

Wash the chicken and steam with a blend of 1 onion, ginger, 2 peppers, aniseed and 1 green pepper and water

Fry the chicken

Slice onions and fry in the oil

Add tomato paste and stir

Blend the remaining onions and add to it

Blend fresh tomatoes and add to it, add the chicken stock and allow to cook

Add shrimp powder and coconut milk, stir and allow to simmer

Add all purpose seasoning and salt to taste

When the stew is ready, scoop some and set aside

Wash your rice and add to the stew in the pot

Stir and add water as you would when cooking rice

Water shouldn't be too much so the rice is not too soft

Allow rice to cook on low heat, stirring occasionally

SALAD

Ingredients

- 1 Cabbage
- 2 large Carrots
- 1 cucumber
- 1 onion
- 1 beetroot
- 1 baked beans
- 2 sardines
- 4 boiled eggs
- 1 Mayonnaise

METHOD

Wash all Vegetables thoroughly with water and vinegar

Slice all vegetables into desired shapes, use a grater or knife, combine

Slice boiled eggs, taking out egg yolks first

Mix egg yolks with 3 tbsps of mayonnaise

Mix with the vegetables

Strain sardine oil and add sardines to the salad, chill and serve or serve fresh

Maame Akosua knows her daughter would enjoy the jollof rice so much. She quickly moves to a personal favorite of hers before Little Akosua decides to eat some jollof instantly.

YAM & 'KONTOMIRE' STEW
'Kontomire' is also known as taro leaves. Where taro leaves are absent, spinach could be used as replacement.
KONTOMIRE STEW
Ingredients
- Kontomire leaves
- Palm oil
- 2 large size onions
- 4 large habanero peppers
- 4 medium size fresh tomatoes
- Salted dried tilapia
- 8 boiled eggs
- Canned Mackerel in tomato sauce
- Smoked Mackerel
- Shrimp powder (optional)

METHOD

Wash kontomire leaves and put in a pan
Peel onions, wash tomatoes and peppers and place on top of the leaves
Wash the dried tilapia and add to it
Pour water into it and put on low heat
Remove onions, tomatoes and peppers and blend
Turn off heat, remove tilapia and strain leaves
Heat palm oil in a pan and fry onions
Pour blended onion mix into it and prepare stew
Sprinkle shrimp powder into the stew
Add smoked mackerel and simmer
Add canned mackerel
Finally grind and add the taro leaves and allow to simmer
Peel boiled eggs and place on top of the stew to serve with yam

BOILED YAM

Ingredients
- **1 tuber of yam**
- **Water**
- **Salt to taste**

METHOD
> **Peel yam and slice into desirable shapes**
> **Wash and add water and salt to taste, boil until soft**
> **Serve with 'Kontomire' stew**

Little Akosua looks ahead and finds her uncles and dad standing around the barbeque grill and she says thank you to her mum and goes to ask them how they made their grilled chicken.

GRILLED CHICKEN

Ingredients

- Soft Chicken pieces
- Onions
- Ginger
- Garlic
- Mayonnaise
- Oil
- Pepper
- Salt
- Seasoning
- Turmeric

METHOD

Wash chicken and pat dry

Lay chicken pieces on grill

Blend all ingredients with oil into a thick paste

Smear on chicken and turn as and when needed, continually smearing while they grill until ready

Finally! The drink bar, with a beautiful setup stood in the corner. Little Akosua can see the drink dispensers "sweating" with melting ice as the delicious drinks are displayed in them.
She runs back to her mum to ask her to tell her all about the mocktails and drinks she sees.

MANGO MOJITO

Ingredients
- Mango Puree 1 cup
- Mint leaves ¼ cup
- Lemon 1
- Soda water 300ml
- Ice cubes 1 cup
- Mojito mint syrup 30ml

METHOD

Blend all ingredients except the syrup and lemon
Pour into a glass, add the mojito syrup, stir
Slice lemon and put into the drink
Serve

PASSION MOJITO

Ingredients

- 1 cup Passion fruit Puree
- Mint leaves ¼ cup
- Lemon 1
- Soda water 300ml
- Ice cube 1 cup
- Mojito mint syrup

METHOD

Blend all ingredients together except lemon and syrup
Stir in syrup and add sliced lemons
Serve

VANILLA MILKSHAKE

Ingredients
- ¼ cup vanilla powder
- ¼ cup condensed milk
- 20ml pop corn syrup
- 90ml full cream milk
- 12 ice cubes

METHOD
Blend all ingredients together
serve

Banana peanut butter Smoothie

Ingredients
- 2 pieces banana
- 30ml plain yoghurt
- ¼ cup peanut butter
- 30ml condensed milk
- 90ml full cream milk
- 10 ice cubes

METHOD
   Blend all ingredients
   Serve

"Mummy, how come there are no snacks to go with these yummy looking drinks?" Little Akosua asked her mum. She tells her to go behind the drink setup and she's pleased to find the snacks the kids requested for.

PEANUT BUTTER BURGER

Ingredients

- Burger buns
- Peanut butter
- Mayonnaise
- Mustard
- Lettuce
- Cabbage
- Cucumber slices
- Minced meat
- Seasoning, salt, black pepper
- Chopped onion pieces
- Chopped habanero pepper pieces
- Sunny side up fried egg
- Grated Mozarella Cheese
- Butter

METHOD

To make burger meat, mix minced meat with seasoning, salt, black pepper, chopped onion pieces and chopped pepper

Form into a ball

Smear butter on a heated skillet and press the meat balls to flatten, allow to cook and brown on one side, turn over and allow other side to cook

Remove them and smear butter over skillet

Place buns on skillet to toast them

ASSEMBLY

Smear peanut butter on bottom buns

Mix mustard and mayonnaise

Place meat on bun, add chopped vegetables and sprinkle cheese cover with sunny side-up omelette

Smear mayo-mustard mix on top buns and use to cover the assembled bun

KELEWELE AND ROASTED PEANUTS

Ingredients

- **Ripe Plantains 5 fingers**
- **Ginger**
- **Dry chilli pepper**
- **Salt**
- **Oil**

METHOD

Peel plantains and wash them

Slice them into small pieces

Grind ginger and pepper with oil into a thick paste

Add salt and pour over the ripe plantains

Stir and allow to sit in the fridge for an hour, or you can fry instantly

Deep fry in hot oil

Serve with nuts

Little Akosua is jumping for joy at this stage. She serves herself some kelewele and dishes extra for her cousins as she heads straight to the main house to announce that the party has began.

The children are excited about the food and drinks. Everyone is happy. Maame Ama is extremely pleased that all turned out well despite the late cancellations as she says a big thank you to Maame Akosua and gives her a big hug.

Maame Akosua smiles and says, "What is family for?"

The birthday girl is grinning from ear to ear as everyone sings a happy birthday for her once more as she cuts her cake. A prayer is offered and they begin to eat all the delicious meals. They dance to tunes playing in the background afterwards.

What a beautiful birthday cookout, certainly turned out better than anticipated.

www.ingramcontent.com/pod-product-compliance
Lightning Source LLC
Chambersburg PA
CBHW040902110726

48005CB00001B/166